Black and White / Schwarz auf Weiß

Erfahrungen aus Südafrika

Norbert Herrmann und Enikö Gömöri

Approaching Johannesburg

Bhoties lining up my way
Sissis everywhere I stay
Family members of such an incredible number
Are nice to have but even encumber
My way along Golden Highway to Johannesburg

Township beauties on Eldorado's streets,
They are in need to eat – right now – not in a week
For even flavoured condoms do not feed
There's so much they have to give
But – will they manage to stay negative?

I turn and I see bombastic Eastgate mall
Shop next to shop, they sell it all
People are lured into this new life's geometry
They celebrate cash's cemetery

Up north I see fear penetrating from the dark outside
Fear that is not telling black from white
Fear that is gluing people together
Making them stay behind huge walls forever

In the metro bus people endlessly preach
They explain the world as they start to speak
Here omniscience is still existent
no matter that no one ever listened

I finally enter the centre, as I cross Gandhi Square
I'm the only white person as I am perfectly aware
Rejecting looks at Jeppe Street taxi rank
Then he starts burbling, the Johannesburg crank

"When you're open-minded, you will find a lot
Welcoming smiles in this ayoba hot spot.
Helping hands, high-rises, politics and the thunder
In Johannesburg you just can't stop to wonder."

EGOLI

Nobody in Soweto

Fast wäre ich ihm über die Füsse gelaufen, beim Soweto Marathon. Er fragt mich, ob denn alles ok sei, es seien immerhin noch 5 Berge vor uns. „Timothy, ich heiße Timothy." „Norbert" schnaufe ich ihm entgegen. „Hä" sagt er, „hä?" „Mein Name ist Norbert. Nor-Bert, wie No-Bird, wie wenn im Himmel kein Vogel ist, No Bird." Eine halbe Stunde später habe ich ihn wieder eingeholt, noch vier Berge vor uns. „Hallo Timothey", diesmal lächele ich. Timothy schaut konfus. „Ich kenne Deinen Namen, ich kenne Deinen Namen" und er fasst sich an die Stirn. „Hallo Nobody!"

From Germany

"How did you come here, where is your guide?" he asks smiling, as we wait for the lift to bring us back down. "Oh, we don't have no guide, we came here unescorted" is our answer. "Ah, I like that very much. It underlines the fact that here in the city it is not that bad as stated in the news." "It was an adventure for us, coming here with our car. But it is all right." "So," he looks at us, "you must be from Germany?" We look blank, while two tourists from Japan approach. They are accompanied by this man, he is their guide. He points at us. "Look, these guys come from Germany. They arrive at the airport, rent a car and go wherever they want, even to Capetown or Port Elisabeth. Or to Downtown Johannesburg to take a look down the 50th floor of Carlton Tower." The two Japanese gaze at us.

13

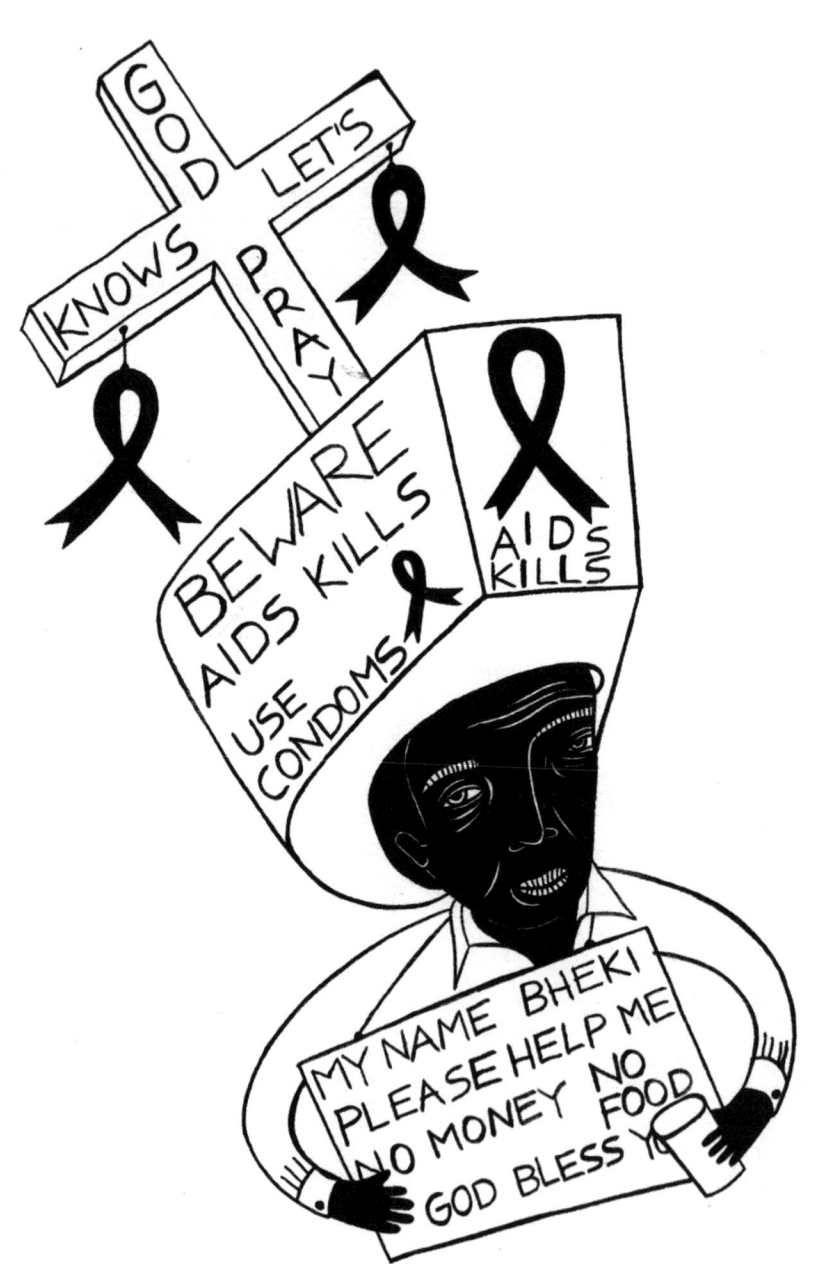

14

Kein Bettler

Er hat mich gesehen, hat mir kurz zugeblinzelt. Oder bilde ich mir das nur ein? Inzwischen wühlt er wieder im Müllbehälter. Doch, jetzt schaut er kurz zu mir. In meiner Hand sind noch die 20 Rand, die ich beim Handeln um die zwei Fußball Shirts gespart habe. 20 Rand! Ich gehe ein paar Schritte, dem Müllsammler hinterher. Der Rücken seiner Jacke ist zerrissen. Seine Hose von Schmutz übersäht. Die Schuhe völlig zerschunden. Ich berühre seine Schulter. Noch einmal. Er dreht sich zu mir, ich strecke ihm den Geldschein entgegen. Er schaut, zu meiner Hand, dann mir in die Augen. Ganz kurz. Er dreht sich weg. Und geht weiter. Ich stecke die 20 Rand in meine Hosentasche. Ich will diesen Schein nicht mehr in meiner Hand halten.

SHOOT
TO
KILL

Niederschläge

Raketenangriffe, Bombeneinschläge ganz in der Nähe. Das gesamte Haus vibriert, mächtiges Dröhnen. Und die Südafrikaner? Als wenn nichts wäre, keine Reaktion. Nur der Nachbar macht das Fenster zu, wegen des Lärms. Er hört Kwaito und schraubt an seinem Fahrrad herum, er will eine Schutzkonstruktion anbringen. Um sich beim Radeln gegen das spritzende Wasser zu schützen. Er ist einer der wenigen, die hier in Johannesburg mit dem Fahrrad zur Arbeit fahren. Und Schutzbleche gibt es hier keine, „Das ist etwas für Europäer," hat man ihm im Bikeshop in Linden gesagt, „Europäer fahren mit dem Rad zur Arbeit, die brauchen ein Schutzblech". Bongani behilft sich also jetzt mit einer von oben nach unten durchgeschnittenen Plastikflasche, die er unter den Sattel schraubt. Diese Konstruktion mag ihn gegen den roten Matsch schützen, der vom Hinterrad hochspritzt. Bongani hat aber noch keine Idee, wie er sich vor dem Dreck schützen kann, der ihm vom Vorderrad ins Gesicht klatscht. Und erst recht nutzt diese Plastikflasche nichts gegen die größte Gefahr im Straßenverkehr in Johannesburg: Taxifahrer. Es scheint, dass die Taxi-Windschutzscheibe einen Filtermechanismus integriert hat, der Fahrradfahrer ausblendet. Gleichzeitig scheint dieser Filter das Umschalten der Ampel auf Grün mit einem Vorsprung von fünf Sekunden anzuzeigen. Die Taxis fahren immer als erstes, wenn die Ampel noch rot ist. Und immer schaltet die Ampel auf grün, sobald die Taxis mitten auf der Kreuzung sind. Bongani behauptet, die Taxis würden durch ihr Losfahren das Umschalten der Ampeln auf Grün erst auslösen. Vor Taxis muss man sich als Fahrradfahrer in Johannesburg besonders in Acht nehmen, im Grunde aber vor allen Kraftfahrzeugen. Es gibt Hügel, Regen, und nach südafrikanischer Logik daraus folgend, keine Fahrradfahrer. Deshalb wissen die motorisierten Verkehrsteilnehmer auch nicht, wie damit umzugehen ist, wenn so ein strampelndes Männlein aus dem Nichts auftaucht.

Jetzt ist das Dröhnen endlos, jetzt knallen die Eisbrocken in Salven vom Himmel. Es scheint eine neue Art von Waffe zu sein, die gerade auf Johannesburg abgefeuert wird. Aber spätestens mit Beginn des Regens kommt die Ahnung, dass das da draußen doch kein Militär- sondern lediglich Niederschlag ist. Ein Gewitter, das wieder quadratmetergrosse Teerflächen aus den Strassen wegspülen wird. Wie Einschlagskrater. Ein nächstes Hinderniss für Fahrradfahrer. „Normal" zeigt der Gesichtsausdruck von Bongani an. Hier in eGoli, wie Johannesburg auf isiZulu genannt wird, heißt es, die Erde sei nicht nur goldgetränkt, die Erde sei auch magnetisch. Unwetter und Blitze würden richtiggehend angezogen und dann entladen die sich mit Krachen, wie Raketeneinschläge.

Regenrad

Ganz durchnässt war ich erst, als mich der GM Hummer überholte, die fahrenden Reifen spritzten literweise Wasser auf meine Hose, mein TShirt, mir ins Gesicht. Ich trat weiter in die Pedalen, bergauf durch den Regen. Einfach stehen bleiben würde mich in dieser Situation nicht voran bringen. Ich dachte daran, zu fluchen, erwartete mir davon aber auch keine Erleichterung. Heulen als Alternative hätte bei diesem Regen kaum Aussenwirkung, die Tränen würden in den Regenmassen einfach untergehen. Mitten in diesen Überlegungen erreichte ich irgendwann doch die Kuppe, immernoch hin und her gerissen ob ich fluchen oder vielleicht doch heulen sollte. Da sah ich die Gestalt zwischen den Autos. Eine Mülltüte übergezogen versuchte er Zeitungen an die Fahrerin und an den Fahrer zu bringen, völlig durchnässte Zeitungen. Als er mich sah lachte er und rief: „Eita my bro, you're fine?" Ein Zucken lief mir übers Gesicht, dann lachte ich zurück „I'm fine".

My Shoes

There is a unique glance in his eyes as he approaches me. "A person like me," he fumbles for words. "A person like me is always suspect." I do not know what to reply. I swallow. I hardly dare to look at him as he faces me. "For people like you" he continues decidedly. "For people like you it is a reasonable strategy to expect the worst when it comes to dealing with people like me." Wasn't there a slight sign of friendliness when he started to speak? Where has that gone? What made his voice turn hostile? His right hand slowly slides, disappears in the buggy pocket of his trousers. I focus on the ground, head down. No movement. "You know," he continues. "I need shoes."

Two days after that I see him sitting in the middle of the robot people. They are chatting, drinking fermented, self-brewed beer. As I pass by he recognizes me. He smiles as he points at his shoes. My shoes.

13 Cent

„Sorry, hier ist Freedom. Genau, der Nachtpförtner. Der mit dem Fahrrad, genau. Danke, es geht mir gut. Ja, meine Frau ist noch in Simbabwe. Entschuldigung dass ich so spät bei Ihnen anrufe. Hoffentlich haben Sie nicht schon geschlafen. Ich brauche Hilfe. Ich war heute abend zu spät hier zur Arbeit. Mein Fahrrad ist kaputt. Der Reifen ist geplatzt. Als ich über den Bordstein gefahren bin. Deshalb musste ich den Bus nehmen, der kommt spät. Deshalb war ich heute nicht pünktlich da zur Arbeit. Der Reifen vom Fahrrad ist jetzt platt, aber den repariere ich morgen, wenn ich nach Hause komme. Sorry dass ich anrufe, ich hoffe Sie haben noch nicht geschlafen. Ich bin heute mit dem Bus gekommen, morgen früh muss ich wieder den Bus nach Hause nehmen. Aber leider habe ich nicht genügend Geld dabei für den Bus zurück nach Hause. Deshalb rufe ich an. Entschuldigung, ich brauche noch 13 Cent für die Rückfahrt."

Parkbesuch

Er könne auch die Polizei rufen. Er sei hier der Park-
wächter und wenn es sein muss, dann ruft er die Polizei.
Ob denn nun wirklich alles in Ordnung wäre mit mir.
Aber ich sitze doch nur im Gras, auf der Wiese, und
lese. „Everything allright" sage ich jetzt zum dritten
mal. Er schaut mir direkt in die Augen, versucht, mich
mit seinem Blick zu erforschen. Ich schüttele den Kopf.
Er gibt auf, dreht sich weg. Ganz langsam trottet er
weiter, in Richtung einer Gruppe von Schwarzen, die
unter einem Baum liegen, sich dort lautstark unter-
halten. Er wendet sich noch einmal um zu mir, dem
einzigen Weissen im Park, und zuckt mit den Schultern.

POSITIVE LIVING

Kalt ists

„Eine Jacke würde mir helfen" sagt Pumla. Sie streicht mit ihren vergilbten Fingern über den warmen Pullover des Mannes und nickt. „Es ist kalt, wie kalt es ist." Der Mann fasst Pumlas Jacke an. Wie dünn die ist. Pumla legt nach: „Und Socken, Socken für Großvater und mich." Die zwei Rand, die der Mann ihr gab, läßt sie nebenbei in der Tasche ihrer dünnen Jacke verschwinden. Der Mann dreht sich zum Gehen. Er kann nicht die ganze Welt retten, auch nicht Pumla, oder? „Die Socken, nicht vergessen!" ruft Pumla ihm hinterher. „Ja" murmelt der Mann, „Pumla hat recht. Kalt ist es."

Bustanz

Irgend einer der Busse könnte doch anhalten. Nur einer. Hier stehe ich, mache den vorbeifahrenden Busfahrern Handzeichen: Faust nach unten, Zeigefinger nach oben; ich zwinkere, winke, dreh mich im Kreis. Aber meinen Bustanz interessiert keine Sau. Nur der Mann im blauen Overall auf der anderen Strassenseite schaut verdutzt. Wie komm ich in einen dieser Busse rein, ich will doch nur zur Arbeit, wirklich. Zwei Chancen habe ich, genau zwei Chancen. Entweder der Bus hält zufällig genau hier wo ich stehe, um Leute aussteigen zu lassen, da kann ich dann schnell hineinhüpfen. Oder ich finde wie gestern und vorgestern wieder eine Einheimische, die für mich den Bus stoppt. Aber fragt mich nicht, wie die das macht! Die steht nur da, wie ich jetzt dastehe und tut genau das, was ich seit einer viertel Stunde mache, sie senkt die Faust nach unten. Für sie stoppt der Bus.

Mittagspause

Das war meine bisher grösste Herausforderung hier in Südafrika. Ich begleitete Moses und Luzuko auf ihrem Weg zum Mittagessen. Für mich ist es normaler Weise ein Fussweg von 10 Minuten zum Shoppingcenter, aber zusammen mit Luzuko und Moses war es anders. Die beiden Jungs liefen langsam, wirklich langsam. Langsam in der ausführlichsten Bedeutung des Wortes Langsam. Für mich erinnerte das eher an „zielgerichtetes Stehen". Als ich das Schweigen brach und darauf hinwies, dass die Mittagspause lediglich eine Stunde lang sei, schauten sie einander an und bewegten mal wieder eines ihrer Beine. „Diese Deutschen" hörte ich Luzuko sagen „die rennen ununterbrochen." Ich beruhigte mich, ich wollte nicht der Deutsche sein. Zwischen meinen Schritten zählte ich bis 10, das half. Später zählte ich bis 50. Aber ich muss schon sagen, ich hatte ein Loch im Bauch bis wir im Shoppingcenter waren. Mit den beiden werde ich nie wieder zum Mittagessen gehen. Und Moses und Luzuko nie wieder mit mir.

ONE WIFE ENOUGH

Wellblechhütte

„Shack" schreibt der Reporter in seinen Notizblock. Und er fragt nochmal nach: „Wellblechhütte?" Benson nickt. Benson hat sogar eine elektrische Heizung in seinem Shack, aber kein fließendes Wasser. Bei der jetztigen Kälte würden die Leitungen sowieso einfrieren. Der Reporter schaut auf. Benson erklärt. Dass er eine Heizung hat heisst nicht, dass es warm ist in seiner Wellblechhütte. Und das nicht nur wegen der unzureichenden Wärmeisolierung. Wenn mal wieder öffentliche Stromleitungen gestohlen werden, weil die Kupferrohre wertvoll sind, dann gibt es für Benson ein paar Nächte lang keinen Strom, keine Heizung, keine TV-Übertragung von der WM, kein elektrisches Licht und keinen heißen Tee. Diesmal schaut der Reporter nicht auf, er unterstreicht aber in seinen Aufzeichnungen das Wort „Shack", dreifach.

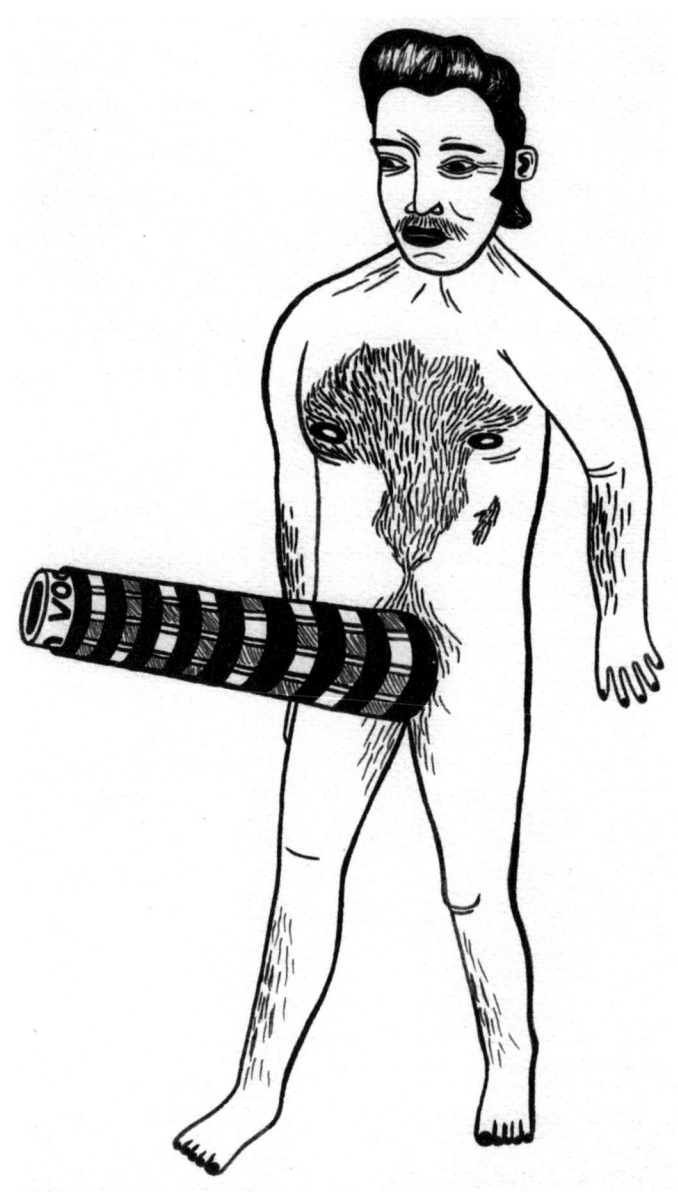

Ponte

"We nearly made it into," Paul says, his eyes glancing. "We nearly made it. We were driving through the suburbs, in high spirits, Ponte coming into our mind. Even if it was nighttime, we found the entrance to the parking lot. The guard there advised us not to drive into the lot, the car wouldn't be safe there. So we asked whether it was safe to park outside the lot. 'Not safe', he replied, 'but safer'. Finally he proposed to have an eye on our car, parking directly in front of his guards box. And on we went to Ponte front door. Half past eleven. Another guard. 'Just for five minutes', we asked 'just having a look, just once taking the lift.' He looked at us, five brave, strong, white guys. He thought, whatever has to be thought in that moment. 'No' was his answer. It was a kind of 'no' I never heard before." Paul looks into our eyes, not a wink, just straight into our eyes. "I strongly believe he saved our lives."

KILLS
99,9 %
OF
GERMS

Nachtstrasse

„Fahr!" schreit sie mich an. Etwas verstört wende ich meinen Kopf zu ihr, was ist in meine Freundin gefahren? Da sehe ich aus dem Augenwinkel die männliche Gestalt, seelenruhig taxiert er durch das Seitenfenster den Rücksitz unseres Autos. Muss sich in dieser gott-verlassenen Gegend aus dem toten Winkel angeschlichen haben. „Jetzt fahr!" Ganz kurz nur schaue ich rechts und links, dann gebe ich Gas, über die rote Ampel. „Vielleicht wollte er einfach nur betteln" versuche ich zu beruhigen. Meine Freundin und ich schauen uns an, ihr Gesicht wird von den Strassenlaternen nur schwach beschienen. „Vielleicht."

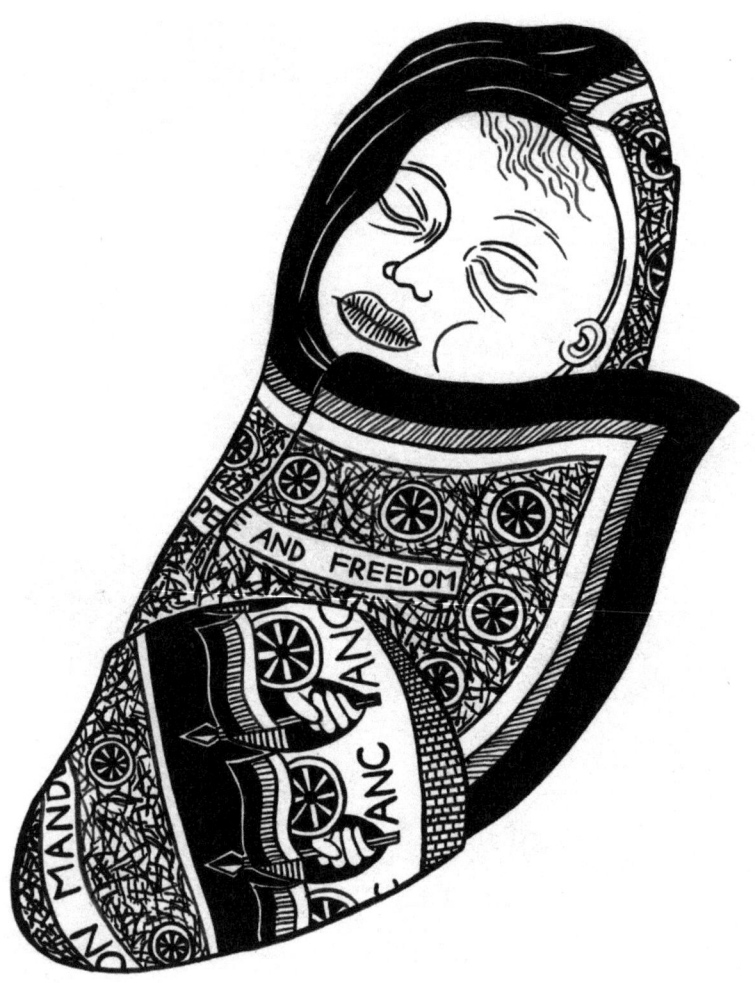

Leaving Jozi

Europe. This is where I am heading to. Back to country-wide good education, national roads without potholes, astonishing art exhibitions. I already picture Claude Monet's "water lilies" which I will see in Paris. It is an impressionistic masterpiece, transforming reality – water lilies – into a feeling. Horizontal waters mirroring vertical skies, no horizon. Monet had a gardener only taking care for his water lilies.

On my last walk to the Gautrain station at Rosebank I pass gardeners, caretakers, and watchmen. They keep staring at the big bags I carry. Yes, again, I feel intimidated. All I want to do is walk, walk through the city that I have called my home for more than two years. And then catch the train to the airport. Straight in front of me, less than 5 km away, I see the downtown high rises, vivid Hillbrow, shrouded in legend Ponte City, the top of the top of Carlton tower. I remember my excitement when strolling through the areas of Central Business District for the first time. For this trip I left my purse and my cell phone at home, cached 50 Rand into my pocket to jump on a Metro bus heading downtown. Crowded streets, market stands – so much different to northern suburb reality, so different to Rosebank.

Now again, above that fantastic downtown skyline, I see the South African sky. Once more I am stunned: this topology, this dimension of clouds. It looks like a mega-screen movie in 3D, transforming abstraction into feeling, sometimes resampling real forms. Yes,

I admit, it looks better than Monets' water lilies.
I pass walls and fences, security-cameras. Oh my god
how I will enjoy walking through German streets, at
night, a bottle of cold beer in my hand, without any
fear of being mugged. I encountered South Africans
who laugh at people that were mugged. "Stay in your
house" is what they would tell. "Stay in your prison" is
what I would hear. Malls. That's the public part of the
prison, the area that South Africans consider as freedom. Those malls are unique in this continent. One
of the reasons why South Africa might be rated as not
being part of "Real Africa", shifting South Africa closer
to Europe and US. White people around, the "white
factor", that's another argument for Milisuthando Bon-
gela in her weekly Mail&Guardian column to explain
why South Africans think their country is better off
than other African countries. Another uniqueness for
Africa: 6-lane highways between Joburg and the Capital
Pretoria. But then: potholes and potholes between East
London and Blomfontein, on the National Route N6.
And potholes besides my pavement on Oxford Road.
The Gautrain bus passes by. Hardly a passenger inside.
Who wants to pay double the prize of the Metro bus
fare? "Financial apartheit" I heard a colleague saying
once. He remembered buses from decades ago. While
he had to queue for an hour to catch a crowded bus to
his township these whity buses went nearly empty. But
this is history, now at least Putco and Metro buses take
all passengers, even if a white person in a Metro bus

still seems something special. Whites being infected by HIV are also extraordinary – and it is hard to find the statistics that separate by ethnic groups. There is no easy explanation for the spread of the epidemic in black South Africa. Multi partnerships is considered one outstanding accelerator of HIV. But no way to cut that down; even role models celebrate their multi-partnership life. Why should the citizen of – let's say the township of Mamalodi – then go for single partnership or at least for condomizing? Because when condomizing he would defend the prosperous future that he or she is far from expecting? No, to get the future right, people say: I'll make a plan. I'll make a plan. I'll make a plan. This powerful poet from Orange Farm comes into my mind. Dazzling words hip-hopping out his ever-creative brain. An enlightened person, I still consider him to be this country's future. And – as soon as his girlfriend unexpectedly became pregnant he started collecting for lobola. Culture catches everybody here in South Africa. I also remember my confusion when I saw these adverts on downtown and township streets that are touting "penis enlargement" and "same day abortion" on the same placard. Keeping in mind that especially in South African townships violence against women is worldwide top in statistics. That's how I learn that in South Africa contradictions coexist powerfully and might even strengthen one another. Just look at the ever blooming security sector.

"Do you like South Africa?" was the frequent question

when people found out about my status. I learned from the answers of other foreigners what I was expected to reply: beautiful landscape, amazing beaches, Drakensberge, Capetown, the weather – did anybody ever mention the people? What really got into my mind was: "Yes, the weather is nice – but do not forget about these spontaneous Jozi rainfalls and artillery thunders, attacking you out of blue skies. Yes, and the landscape is beautiful. But remember, Europe has a lot of beautiful landscapes too. And you can easily reach them with public transport, you can fearlessly walk through city centres, you don't need to be endlessly grappling with your alarm system. Yes, I like South Africa, but – this is not my dream of a country." If I wrote something critical like that about South Africa people would then comment: "Why are you here?" – maybe after looking at my name to find out whether I am black or white. Why am I here? Good question.

A friend exercised for long distance running in the Joburg Northern Suburbs streets. He experienced people proactively looking at him, keen on greeting with the unquestioned "fine and you". After the Worldcup Jozi people would have lost their proactive willingness to greet passers-by. But meanwhile that would have changed back. Whereas in Capetown I felt as a disturbing person when exercising, I received a lot of unfriendly looks and was greeted only reluctantly. Running East London, people just ignored this white person, nor friendly neither unfriendly, just indifferent. That was one point when I re-learned: in South Africa it never is appropriate to talk about "people". Differences are ethnic and financial, differences are in talent and in opportunity, differences are in self awareness, difference is everywhere. And generalization would only lead to conflict, because in South Africa you most easily will find proof for opposing arguments.

Some questions remain: Why do some people not lock the door when visiting a public toilet? Why do some people complain about crime and in the same sentence say they would love their country? Why isn't more money spent on the schooling system? I remember, after reading in his newspaper about the national matric results 2009 some person called this country "brain-low nation".

People on the streets hardly ever get the chance to leave this country. South Africa rather absorbs more and more people from other African countries. If I was to imagine Europe conceiving all these immigrants, there would be high chances of xenophobia – also in Europe not everybody welcomes foreigners as source of fresh brain. In this case I think that South Africa is doing a damn good job compared to "first world" countries – even if here's still needs for enhancements. I notice a surprising level of social peace in South Africa – considering the colonial and the apartheit history, considering the huge gaps in income, considering the temptations of corruption. South Africa copes with having the first and the third world within its own boundaries. Whereas Europe desperately tries to keep the third world out of its boundaries – by means of huge walls and fences and security cameras – and rude laws. The moment I enter the Gautrain station I figure it out: to me South Africa feels like a real world with all its distinct contrasts. Thus it is a model to learn from. Maybe in Europe continental fences cannot be kept forever, maybe a kind of "third world" will upraise within the "first world". Then Europe would need to cope with this, and I am not sure whether Europe will do better than South Africa does now. That's the feeling which the South African reality made me aware of. To understand that, to get rid of European arrogance, that's the reason why I was here. As the Gautrain doors close smoothly it feels like being back in Europe – within South Africa.

Enikö Gömöri und Norbert Herrmann

haben Johannesburg aufgezeichnet. Visuell und textuell und in Ausschnitten, in subjektiven, zufälligen Ausschnitten. Die Zusammenstellung ist damit eine persönliche und kann keine exemplarische sein für das unüberschaubare Johannesburg. Jeder der Johannesburg gesehen hat, weiß, in dieser Stadt – wie im ganzen Land Südafrika – gibt es nichts, was als exemplarisch gelten könnte.

Zwischen 2009 und 2011 lebten Enikö Gömöri und Norbert Herrmann im Bezirk Illovo in Johannesburg. Mit Bus, Bahn, Taxi, Fahrrad, VW Käfer und zu Fuß lernten sie Downtown und Uptown, Townships und Villenviertel, Straßenmärkte und Shopping-Centren kennen. Und Menschen.

Enikö Gömöri ist Illustratorin und Grafikerin, Norbert Herrmann ist Schriftsteller und Podcaster und arbeitet als Projektmanager. In Südafrika unterstützte er über zwei Jahre eine HIV-Vorsorgeorganisation für Jugendliche und begleitete eine Gruppe von jungen Slammern.

Links

tuneplaces.com/johannesburg
enikogomori.com
skytoradio.blogspot.com

Inhaltsangabe

Alle visuellen Arbeiten stammen aus der Reihe
„Black and White / Schwarz auf Weiß", 2010–2011
Tusche auf Papier